HOW TO STARTS FOOD TRUCK BUSINESS

"Rolling Success: A Step-by-Step Guide to Launching Your Own Food Truck Business"

Vanessa Anderson

TABLE OF CONTENTS

INTRODUCTION

Welcome to the world of food truck entrepreneurship, a journey filled with sizzling grills, savory aromas, and the joy of serving up culinary delights on wheels. In this book, we'll embark on a practical exploration of how to start and thrive in the food truck business – no frills, just the nitty-gritty essentials that turn dreams into reality.

My own journey into the world of food trucks began with a simple yet profound realization. Picture this: a bustling street, the aroma of exotic spices lingering in the air, and a small food truck dishing out mouthwatering treats. It wasn't just about the food; it was about the freedom to bring unique flavors to diverse corners of the community.

As I stood in line, awaiting my turn for a delicious meal, I knew I wanted to be part of this vibrant world. That experience ignited a passion to demystify the process of starting a food truck business – to break it down into manageable steps for anyone with a culinary dream and the drive to roll it into reality.

In these pages, I'll share practical insights, lessons learned from the road, and essential tips to guide you on your food truck journey. But before we dive into the details, remember this: it all starts with a simple spark, just like the one that fueled my own adventure.

Now, let's fire up those engines, embrace the delicious possibilities, and turn your food truck dreams into a reality that hits the road. Your journey begins here.

Call to Action:

Hungry for your own adventure? Turn the page and join me on this culinary expedition. Discover the roadmaps to success, learn from the pitfalls, and uncover the savory secrets that will set your food truck business on a course for triumph. The journey is yours for the taking – are you ready to roll?

Chapter 1: The Allure of Food Truck Entrepreneurship

The enticing world of food truck entrepreneurship beckons with the promise of freedom, creativity, and the ability to take your culinary creations directly to the streets. In this chapter, we'll explore the undeniable allure of starting your own food truck business and help you determine if it's the right path for you.

Is a Food Truck Business Right for You?

Before you dive into the world of food trucks, let's take a moment to assess if it aligns with your goals and lifestyle. Practical Tip: Consider your passion for food, willingness to embrace a mobile lifestyle, and your entrepreneurial spirit. This self-reflection is the first step in determining if the food truck life suits you.

Crafting Your Culinary Concept

Crafting a successful food truck business begins with a solid culinary concept. This section guides you through the crucial steps of identifying your niche and researching market trends to create a concept that not only satisfies taste buds but also captures the attention of your target audience.

Identifying Your Niche:

Pinpoint the unique flavors or cuisine that sets your food truck apart. Practical Tip: Consider your personal culinary strengths, local preferences, and potential gaps in the market to identify a niche that resonates with your passion and potential customers.

Researching Market Trends:

Stay ahead of the curve by researching current food trends in your area. Practical Tip: Attend local food festivals, follow social media food communities, and engage with potential customers to understand what's in demand. This research will shape your menu and keep you competitive.

Navigating Legalities and Regulations

To ensure a smooth journey for your food truck, understanding and navigating legalities and regulations is paramount. This section covers the essentials, including permits and licenses, as well as health and safety compliance.

Permits and Licenses 101:

Unpack the paperwork needed to legally operate your food truck. Practical Tip: Develop a checklist of required permits and licenses specific to your location, and establish a timeline for obtaining them to avoid delays in launching your business.

Health and Safety Compliance:

Prioritize the well-being of your customers by adhering to health and safety regulations. Practical Tip: Implement best practices for food handling, storage, and cleanliness. Regularly check and maintain equipment to ensure it meets health standards.

Chapter 2: Designing Your Food Truck

Your food truck is not just a vehicle; it's a rolling kitchen, a mobile eatery, and a visual representation of your culinary identity. This chapter dives into the crucial aspects of designing your food truck for both functional efficiency and eye-catching appeal.

Functional Layouts for Efficiency:

Maximize your food truck's limited space by designing a layout that enhances efficiency. Practical Tip: Consider the workflow of your kitchen – place high-traffic items within easy reach and design a logical flow from prep to service, ensuring a smooth operation during busy periods.

Eye-Catching Branding and Signage:

Your food truck's branding is the first taste customers get of your culinary identity. Practical Tip: Invest in a memorable and legible logo, and ensure your signage is clear and visible. Use vibrant colors and engaging graphics that reflect the spirit of your brand.

Chapter 3: Sourcing Ingredients and Supplies

The quality of your ingredients directly impacts the flavor and success of your culinary creations. This section provides insights into building relationships with suppliers and managing inventory for profitability.

Building Relationships with Suppliers:

Establish reliable and consistent partnerships with suppliers for fresh, high-quality ingredients. Practical Tip: Communicate your specific needs, build a rapport with suppliers, and explore local options to support the community and reduce transportation costs.

Managing Inventory for Profitability:

Effective inventory management is the key to minimizing waste and maximizing profits. Practical Tip: Implement a system for tracking inventory levels, set par levels for ingredients, and regularly review and adjust your inventory strategy based on sales trends.

Chapter 4: Pricing Your Culinary Creations

Setting the right prices for your menu items requires a delicate balance between covering costs and offering value to customers. This section explores the intricacies of costing your menu items and employing competitive pricing strategies.

Costing Your Menu Items:

Calculate the true cost of each menu item, considering ingredients, labor, and overhead. Practical Tip: Factor in both fixed and variable costs to ensure accurate pricing. This clarity will guide you in setting prices that are both competitive and profitable.

Competitive Pricing Strategies:

Position your food truck competitively in the market without compromising profitability. Practical Tip: Research the pricing strategies of similar food trucks in your area, and consider offering combo deals, specials, or loyalty programs to attract and retain customers.

Hitting the Road: Choosing Locations

Taking your food truck on the road requires strategic decisions regarding where to set up shop. This chapter delves into the importance of understanding your target audience, navigating local events and festivals, and making the most of your chosen locations.

Understanding Your Target Audience:

Identify the demographics and preferences of your ideal customers. Practical Tip: Conduct surveys, engage with your community, and analyze data to gain insights into the types of locations and events that align with your target audience.

Navigating Local Events and Festivals:

Participating in local events and festivals can be a game-changer. Practical Tip: Research and secure spots at events that attract your target audience. Build relationships with event organizers for future opportunities.

Chapter 5: Marketing and Promoting Your Food Truck

Effective marketing is essential for attracting customers to your mobile kitchen. This section covers creating an online presence and engaging social media strategies to boost your food truck's visibility.

Creating an Online Presence:

Establish a digital footprint through a user-friendly website and online platforms. Practical Tip: Include your menu, schedule, and contact information. Consider an online ordering system for added convenience.

Engaging Social Media Strategies:

Leverage the power of social media to connect with your audience. Practical Tip: Regularly post engaging content, share behind-the-scenes glimpses, run promotions, and respond promptly to customer interactions.

Managing Finances and Budgeting

Sound financial management is the backbone of a successful food truck business. This section guides you through budgeting for start-up costs and provides insights into tracking expenses and profits.

Budgeting for Start-up Costs:

Plan and allocate your financial resources wisely from the beginning. Practical Tip: Detail all start-up expenses, including permits, equipment, and initial inventory. Create a realistic budget to avoid financial surprises.

Tracking Expenses and Profits:

Implement a robust tracking system to monitor your financial health. Practical Tip: Utilize accounting software to record expenses and revenue. Regularly review financial reports to make informed business decisions.

Chapter 6: Customer Service Excellence

Building a loyal customer base requires exceptional customer service. This section explores strategies for fostering customer loyalty and handling challenges with grace.

Building a Loyal Customer Base:

Provide a memorable experience to turn first-time customers into regulars. Practical Tip: Offer loyalty programs, discounts, or special promotions to express appreciation for repeat business.

Handling Challenges with Grace:

Address customer concerns and challenges calmly and professionally. Practical Tip: Establish a clear process for handling complaints, and view challenges as opportunities to improve and strengthen customer relationships.

Maintenance and Repairs

Keeping your food truck in top condition is essential for smooth operations. This section covers routine maintenance tips and troubleshooting common issues.

Routine Maintenance Tips:

Implement a regular maintenance schedule to prevent breakdowns. Practical Tip: Check equipment, inspect the vehicle, and address minor issues promptly to avoid more significant problems.

Troubleshooting Common Issues:

Equip yourself with the knowledge to address common challenges on the road. Practical Tip: Create a troubleshooting guide for quick reference, and ensure all team members are familiar with basic problem-solving techniques.

Chapter 7: Expanding Your Food Truck Business

As your food truck gains traction, this chapter explores opportunities for expansion, including franchising possibilities and diversifying your culinary offerings to cater to a broader audience.

Franchising Opportunities:

Consider the potential of franchising to replicate your success in new locations. Practical Tip: Develop a comprehensive franchise model, including operational guidelines, branding standards, and ongoing support structures for franchisees.

Diversifying Your Culinary Offerings:

Expand your menu to capture a diverse customer base. Practical Tip: Conduct market research to identify additional menu items that align with your brand. Introduce new offerings gradually and assess customer response.

Learning from Successful Food Truck Entrepreneurs

Drawing insights from those who have successfully navigated the challenges of the food truck industry is invaluable. This section features interviews and insights from accomplished food truck entrepreneurs, providing practical lessons from their experiences on the road.

Interviews and Insights:

Learn from the journeys of successful food truck entrepreneurs through firsthand accounts. Practical Tip: Extract actionable advice and strategies from their stories that resonate with your business goals.

Lessons from the Road:

Reflect on the collective wisdom gained by entrepreneurs who have weathered the challenges. Practical Tip: Identify common themes and lessons that can be applied to your own food truck business, fostering continuous improvement.

Chapter 8: Learning Simple Food Recipes for Your Food Truck Business

In your journey to start a successful food truck business, honing your culinary skills is essential. This chapter focuses on practical steps to learn simple recipes, specifically targeting smoothies and juices. The tone is straightforward, ensuring that all readers can easily grasp the concepts without getting bogged down by complex jargon.

Practice Makes Perfect

Before launching your food truck, dedicate time to practicing your cooking skills. Experiment with different ingredients, techniques, and flavor combinations. This hands-on experience will not only boost your confidence but also help you refine your recipes for the food truck menu.

Practical Tip: Set aside regular time slots for practice sessions. Consistency is key in mastering any skill.

Start with the Basics: Simple Smoothies

Begin your culinary journey with simple smoothie recipes. Choose a variety of fruits, vegetables, and liquids to create a balanced and refreshing drink. Focus on mastering the blending process to achieve the desired consistency.

Practical Tip: Invest in a high-quality blender. It will make the preparation smoother and ensure a consistent texture for your smoothies.

Mastering Juice Combinations

Learning to make fresh and flavorful juices is another valuable skill for your food truck business. Experiment with different fruit and vegetable combinations to create unique and appealing flavors. Understanding the balance between sweetness and acidity is crucial.

Practical Tip: Consider seasonal ingredients for your juices. This not only enhances flavor but also allows you to capitalize on fresh, locally available produce.

Perfecting Presentation

The visual appeal of your food and drinks is as important as the taste. Practice presenting your smoothies and juices in an eye-catching manner. Experiment with garnishes, glassware, and colors to make your offerings stand out.

Practical Tip: Take photos of your creations during practice sessions. This will not only help you refine the presentation but also serve as promotional material for your food truck.

Gather Feedback

Invite friends, family, and potential customers to taste your creations. Pay attention to their feedback and be open to making adjustments. Constructive criticism during the learning phase is invaluable for refining your recipes.

Practical Tip: Create a simple feedback form to gather specific comments on taste, presentation, and overall experience.

By dedicating time to practice, starting with simple recipes, and incorporating practical tips, you'll be well on your way to mastering the culinary skills needed for a successful food truck business.

Chapter 9: Teaming Up – Staffing for Your Food Truck Business

Starting a food truck business is an exciting venture, but it's crucial to recognize that you can't do it all alone. This chapter delves into the importance of having a small team to help run your business smoothly. The tone is straightforward, making it easy for all readers to grasp the essentials without diving into complex jargon.

Understanding the Need for Staff

As a food truck owner, wearing multiple hats is inevitable. However, having 1 to 2 staff members can significantly ease the workload and enhance the overall efficiency of your business. From taking orders to preparing food and managing customers, a team provides essential support.

Practical Tip: Identify tasks that take up most of your time and consider delegating those responsibilities to your staff. This allows you to focus on aspects of the business that require your direct attention.

Selecting the Right Team Members

When hiring staff for your food truck, look for individuals who share your passion for the business and understand the fast-paced nature of the industry. Effective communication and a willingness to learn are key attributes to prioritize.

Practical Tip: Conduct thorough interviews to assess not only the skills of potential candidates but also their ability to work well under pressure and adapt to the dynamic environment of a food truck.

Training for Success

Once you've assembled your team, invest time in proper training. Ensure that your staff is familiar with the menu, food preparation methods, and customer service protocols. This not only guarantees a smooth operation but also enhances the overall customer experience.

Practical Tip: Create a comprehensive training manual that covers all aspects of your food truck operation. This serves as a valuable resource for your staff and helps maintain consistency in service.

Establishing Clear Roles and Responsibilities

Define specific roles and responsibilities for each team member. Whether it's taking orders, handling cash transactions, or preparing food, a clear delineation of tasks minimizes confusion and ensures that everyone knows their part in the operation.

Practical Tip: Use a visual chart or checklist to outline daily tasks. This provides a quick reference for your staff, promoting a well-organized workflow.

Fostering Team Communication

Effective communication is the backbone of a successful food truck operation. Encourage an open dialogue among your team members. Regular team meetings and check-ins create a supportive environment where everyone can voice concerns, share ideas, and collaborate.

Practical Tip: Implement a communication system, whether it's a group chat or a whiteboard in the truck, to keep everyone informed about daily specials, changes, or important updates.

By recognizing the need for a small but efficient team, selecting the right individuals, providing thorough training, establishing clear roles, and fostering effective communication, you'll be well on your way to running a thriving food truck business. Remember, a well-coordinated team enhances not only the efficiency of your operation but also the overall enjoyment of the food truck journey.

CONCLUSION

As you reach milestones in your food truck journey, this concluding chapter celebrates achievements and sets the stage for the ongoing adventure ahead.

Celebrating Milestones:

Acknowledge and celebrate the milestones you've achieved along the way. Practical Tip: Organize events, promotions, or collaborations to involve your community and loyal customers in your celebrations.

Looking Ahead: The Ongoing Journey:

The journey doesn't end; it transforms into a continuous path of growth and innovation. Practical Tip: Set new goals, embrace emerging trends, and stay attuned to customer feedback to ensure a vibrant and evolving food truck business.